THE
BIRTH
of
FREEDOM

PARTICIPANT'S GUIDE

THE
BIRTH
of
FREEDOM

PARTICIPANT'S GUIDE

HOW BIBLICAL FOUNDATIONS
CHANGED HISTORY

JONATHAN AND AMANDA WITT

ZONDERVAN®   ACTONINSTITUTE

ZONDERVAN.com/
AUTHORTRACKER
follow your favorite authors

ZONDERVAN

The Birth of Freedom Participant's Guide
Copyright © 2010 by Acton Institute

Requests for information should be addressed to:
Zondervan, *Grand Rapids, Michigan 49530*

ISBN 978-0-310-32959-6

Cover design: John Hamilton Design
Cover photography: Randy Faris/CORBIS
Interior design: Melissa Elenbaas

Printed in the United States of America

10 11 12 13 14 15 16 17 18 /DCI/ 23 22 21 20 19 18 17 16 15 14 13 12 11 10 9 8 7 6 5 4 3 2 1

Without morals a republic cannot subsist any length of time; they therefore who are decrying the Christian religion, whose morality is so sublime and pure ... are undermining the solid foundation of morals, the best security for the duration of free governments.

CHARLES CARROLL,
signer of the
Declaration of Independence

CONTENTS

This participant's guide explores issues raised in the seven sessions of *The Birth of Freedom* video study. If you plan to lead a group study, a good approach is to watch a given video session and review the corresponding content in this guide before the group meets. The video sessions are relatively easy to digest, so this isn't essential. But reflecting on the material beforehand could make for a more searching and profitable class.

PARTICIPANT'S GUIDE CONTENTS

This participant's guide contains seven sessions corresponding to the seven video sessions:

1. **A Civilization without Slaves:** Slavery was universal until Christendom gradually abolished slavery on the European continent. The rich still abused the poor all too often, but slavery gradually developed into serfdom and serfs eventually became free peasants. This sea change was driven by the idea that every human is made in the image of God.
2. **The Quest for Political Freedom:** Athens and Rome experimented with representative government, but they lacked something that Medieval Europe had: the Judeo-Christian worldview.
3. **The Myth of the Dark Ages:** The European Middle Ages was not a dark, stagnant period. It was a time of amazing technological, economic, and artistic progress—and Christianity played a central role.
4. **Pilgrims' Progress:** In a period stretching from the invention of the printing press through the American Revolution, political and religious freedom continued to grow. Again, Christianity was a driving force.

5. **The Abolitionists:** Medieval Europe got rid of slavery, but it returned in the sixteenth century after Europeans mastered the craft of sailing the high seas. This session traces the struggle to end colonial slavery, first among the English through the unflagging work of Christian statesman William Wilberforce, and later in the United States.

6. **A Tale of Two Revolutions:** The American Revolution led to gradually increasing freedom. The French Revolution led to bloody internal purges and the military dictatorship of Napoleon Bonaparte. What made the difference? The American Revolution embraced its Christian heritage. The French Revolution rejected it.

7. **Relativism vs. Religion:** Some believe that relativism is the best way to defend freedom, but really it's the worst way. Without moral absolutes we have no solid way to refute the contrary opinion of a Stalin or Hitler. Freedom's best guardian, rather, is the shared understanding that we are all made in the image of a good and reasonable Creator.

Each session contains five parts:

Introduction

This section briefly discusses the key scriptural insights related to the session topic.

Video Teaching Notes

This short section lists some of the key themes from the video session along with some white space for notes.

Video Discussion

The discussion questions in this section focus on the material in the video lesson, specific areas of Scripture connected to the video session's themes, and encourage personal application and action.

Bonus Study

This section provides additional discussion material, much of it related to the DVD bonus material that follows each video lesson. This section can be used for group discussion if there is additional time, but can also be viewed between the sessions for further study. It is particularly well suited for more intensive educational settings, such as a high school history class or a church adult education class that stretches over an entire quarter.

Closing Prayer

This section offers some prayer ideas related to the session's key spiritual themes.

SESSION *One*

A CIVILIZATION WITHOUT SLAVES

So God created man in his own image, in the image of God he created him; male and female he created them.

GENESIS 1:27

Each one of us — male and female, young and old — is a uniquely created person of value and inherent worth, made in the image of God.

INTRODUCTION

An obscure Jewish sect in the backwater of the Roman Empire taught that every human being was made in the image of God, and that God loved humanity so much that he sent his son to die on a Roman cross. Eventually, the religion founded upon these beliefs would drive slavery from the continent of Europe.

Freedom from slavery. The freedom to buy, own, and sell property. Freedom of thought, speech, and press. Freedom of religion. The freedom to choose one's occupation. The freedom to vote. The freedom to govern one's own family. The freedom to pursue excellence.

The slow growth of all of these freedoms was helped along by a radical premise: Every human being—man, woman, and child—is made in the image of God and possesses certain unalienable rights.

This idea was foreign to most of the ancient world. It emerged not in Babylon, Greece, or Rome, but in a small, Middle Eastern tribe of people known as the Jews. The Jewish holy writings described a God who fashioned man and woman in his image, giving them inherent value and worth.

And it was a Jewish carpenter, Jesus of Nazareth, who spurred his followers to a fuller understanding of what it means to be made in the image of God. He urged them to treat others—including those of a different gender, ethnicity, or social status—as divine image-bearers, to love them as we would love ourselves. For several centuries, Christ's teachings spread throughout the Roman world and the continent of Europe, a region that would eventually become known simply as *Christendom*.

The history of Christendom is, of course, littered with tragic instances of hypocrisy and oppression; but it is also where political, economic, and religious freedom first took root together and flowered.

Secular history textbooks about the West often overlook the role that Christianity played in this birth of freedom. It's a dangerous omission, for liberty cannot thrive when it is severed from its roots. We must remember the crucial connection between faith and freedom, and teach our children to remember how the idea of freedom was born.

VIDEO TEACHING NOTES

Christianity did not hold civilization back; it drove it forward.

Non-Christian Romans practiced infanticide.

Medieval monasteries preserved and extended civilization.

In the Middle Ages the idea that every human is made in the image of God began influencing every level of society.

Medieval serfs had more rights than Roman slaves.

VIDEO DISCUSSION

1. What does it mean to be free? Some argue that freedom is being able to choose whatever you want to do, a freedom *from* restraint. Others argue that freedom is being *able* to choose what is good and virtuous, which may require limiting our choices. How do these understandings of freedom differ? How would you define "freedom"?

2. This video session looks at how pre-Christian Greek and Roman civilizations viewed certain people as less than fully human. Who were the people they viewed as less than human? In what ways might we treat people as "less than human" today?

3. Often we treat people as "less than human" because we see them as different from ourselves in some way. What are some ways we divide people into classes and categories, assigning a relative value to them? Read Genesis 1:27. How does this verse challenge this way of thinking?

4. What is the relationship between the idea of human equality and human freedom?

> *"You* have never talked to a mere mortal. Nations, cultures, arts, civilization—these are mortal, and their life is to ours as the life of a gnat. But it is immortals whom we joke with, work with, marry, snub, and exploit—immortal horrors or everlasting splendors."
>
> C. S. Lewis, *The Weight of Glory*

5. In the New Testament letter to the Colossians, the apostle Paul advises slaves to serve their masters well, "not only when their eye is on you and to win their favor, but with sincerity of heart and reverence for the Lord" (Colossians 3:22). Some people have accused Paul of accepting a terrible cultural evil. Read Colossians 3:11, Colossians 4:1, and 1 Corinthians 7:21–23. How would you describe his view on slavery after reading these verses?

6. As we saw in the previous question, God's ideal is for Christians to be free from human bondage. Given that this is God's desire for his people, why do you suppose the New Testament writers did not simply condemn slavery outright?

7. When Jesus returned to his hometown synagogue, he was handed the scroll of Isaiah. Opening it, he read a prophecy about his mission: "He has sent me to proclaim freedom for the prisoners and recovery of sight for the blind, to release the oppressed" (Luke 4:18b). Who are those who might be considered prisoners, blind, or oppressed in your community? What are the different ways you might be called to proclaim freedom to them, both spiritually and physically?

BONUS STUDY

If your group has time, you may choose to watch the bonus sections of the video for session one now. (If not, consider viewing them on your own or as a group as part of your between-sessions activities.) Here are some reflection questions for the additional video shorts:

1. The first video short notes how contemporary culture tends to see freedom as freedom from restraint. What kind of freedom do William Allen and Samuel Gregg advocate?

   In what way is merely "doing whatever we want" not true freedom? Can we become slaves to our own whims or appetites? How have you seen this personally in your own life?

   If a person does not believe in objective good, if he thinks "good and evil" are just categories people made up, can such a person be truly free? Why or why not?

2. As the second video short notes, the Judeo-Christian tradition has encouraged an honest, unsparing assessment of our individual and shared history. Can we go overboard with this? If so, how might we balance our assessment with grace and yet not white-wash the past? Give specific examples, if possible.

3. In the third video short, Alan Crippen and Samuel Gregg discuss the apostle Paul's letter to Philemon. With Paul's short letter open in front of you, discuss how Paul both allows for the Roman institution of slavery and powerfully undermines it. Focus especially on verses 15 – 21.

   Also in the third video short, Gregg emphasizes that the Bible doesn't say we are all equally talented or hard-working or should all have an equal standard of living. Rather, the Bible says we are equal in dignity and rights. What problems might arise if Christians assumed that we ought to all have identical advantages?

CLOSING PRAYER

As you close this session, here are some ways you can pray in tune with the themes of today's study:

- Ask God to help you see people the way that he sees them, as individuals he loves.

- Pray that God would help you to recognize ways you may tend to devalue people or treat them with a lack of respect.

- Pray that God would allow you to see your own value in his eyes, as a person he has uniquely made, someone for whom Christ died.

- Ask God for opportunities to speak up on behalf of those who are unable to defend themselves.

SESSION *Two*

THE QUEST FOR POLITICAL FREEDOM

On his robe and on his thigh he has this name written:
KING OF KINGS AND LORD OF LORDS.

REVELATION 19:16

No one, no matter how powerful he may be, is above the law of God. All of us are accountable to our Creator and must give an account to him for our actions.

INTRODUCTION

Christianity taught Medieval Europe that the ruler is not above the higher law of God. The king was not the law. He was the steward of the law.

Civilizations have struggled to check the abuse of power for thousands of years. Anyone who thinks democracy provides the simple cure for this problem should take a closer look at the ancient Athenians. Athens was the great forerunner of American democracy and one of the cradles of Western civilization, and yet it degenerated into a tyranny of the majority.

The execution of the philosopher Socrates is only the most famous instance of what became all too common in Athens: Lacking a firm and widely shared belief in a transcendent moral order, the majority became its own moral order, deciding for themselves what was good and what was evil.

Fortunately, the biblical worldview provides a powerful check against tyranny by teaching everyone—from the peasant to the prince—that God alone is the ultimate standard of morality. Though the kings of Christendom often rationalized their way out of their obligation to rule the people with justice and equity, the spread of Christianity throughout Europe fundamentally changed the status quo. "Because I said so" was no longer a sufficient excuse for a ruler who wished to flout the divine moral order. Even kings were accountable to a higher power. They knew it. Their subjects knew it. And this shared knowledge slowly transformed the political structures of Europe.

VIDEO TEACHING NOTES

Ancient Greek democracy lacked a firm foundation for absolute morality.

Before Constantine, Roman emperors often behaved as if they were the higher law.

When Bishop Ambrose rebuked Theodosius, the Christian emperor repented.

The church insisted on its independence.

The Magna Carta was a seminal victory for human liberty.

VIDEO DISCUSSION

1. According to the video lesson, the Athenian experiment lacked an essential foundation. What was it, and how did this shortcoming manifest itself as ancient Greek democracy began to unravel?

2. Glenn Sunshine and Samuel Gregg discussed an incident late in the fourth century AD: Ambrose, the bishop of Milan, confronted the Roman emperor in broad daylight, telling him to repent of his indiscriminate violence against the city of Thessalonica. A century earlier an emperor in this situation probably would have reacted by having the bishop executed on the spot, yet Emperor Theodosius responded by doing public penance. What changed in Roman culture to allow for such a surprising outcome?

3. Read Psalm 2:10 – 12 and Isaiah 40:22 – 25. If you were a Christian *and* the emperor of ancient Rome, how might these verses speak to you? How would your accountability to God, as a Christian, change the way you would rule over others?

"*If* only no one were ever to acquire material power over others! But to the human being who has faith in some force that holds dominion over all of us, and who is therefore conscious of his own limitations, power is not necessarily fatal. For those, however, who are unaware of any higher sphere, it is a deadly poison. For them there is no antidote."

Aleksandr Solzhenitsyn

4. Many people today say they can't love a God who punishes people for wrongdoing. However, if they were assaulted, or if a loved one were murdered, they would probably want the wrongdoer punished, and not just for revenge. They understand that freedom and the common good can only flourish when justice is upheld. As Christians, how can we emphasize the importance of personal responsibility — of each person facing the consequences of his own actions — and at the same time imitate Christ in forgiving and rehabilitating the wrongdoer?

Which truth do you tend to emphasize more — the need for justice and personal responsibility, or mercy and the need for forgiveness and rehabilitation?

Must we choose between justice and mercy, or can we somehow embrace both? How does the cross of Jesus Christ provide a way of reconciling this tension?

5. Romans 14:12 says that "each of us will give an account of himself to God." This applies to leaders, to ordinary citizens, to the rich, to the poor — everyone. How does your accountability to God affect the way you live your life? How does it affect the way you relate to others?

BONUS STUDY

If your group has time, you may choose to watch the bonus sections of the video for session two now. (If not, consider viewing them on your own or as a group as part of your between-sessions activities.) Here are some reflection questions for the additional video shorts:

1. In the first video short for this session, John Witte Jr. notes that Genesis 1 and 2 teach us that humans are created in the image of God, and that "human dignity is a critical part of the core identity of the person that needs to be protected by human rights." In

other words, human dignity isn't something invented by a human ruler or conferred by the government. Why is this important to remember?

If a people are to achieve ordered liberty, they need to have a positive view of discipline and justice. A right understanding of God encourages both. The God of the Jews is often mischaracterized as a finger-shaking old tyrant who wants to prevent people from having fun and who punishes anyone daring to cross him. How does the biblical picture of God differ from this false caricature? Why is it important that God punishes evil and maintains a consistent standard of justice?

2. In the second video short, Susan Wise Bauer discusses Augustine's idea of two realms or "cities" that rub up against each other here on earth—the city of man, governed by worldly wisdom, and the city of God, a realm that recognizes and is guided by divine authority. What does it look like to live in one of these cities? In which of the cities do you tend to live?

3. In the third video short, Rev. Robert Sirico argues that we must not take our liberty for granted. The nineteenth-century English statesman Lord Acton called liberty "the delicate fruit of a mature civilization." He reminds us that liberty is not the norm in human history but is, in fact, quite rare. What are some of the freedoms that you tend to take for granted? What can we do to avoid taking our liberty for granted?

CLOSING PRAYER

As you close this session, here are some ways you can pray in tune with the themes of today's study:

- Ask God to help you remember that you are accountable for your actions. As Hebrews 4:13 tells us, "Nothing in all creation is hidden from God's sight. Everything is uncovered and laid bare before the eyes of him to whom we must give account."

- Pray that when you are treated unfairly or taken advantage of by another person, you can recognize that God will justly address every wrong and free you from the trap of personal vengeance.

- Ask God to help you understand the harmony of justice and mercy found in the cross of Jesus.

SESSION *Three*

THE MYTH OF THE DARK AGES

The man who had received the five talents went at once and put his money to work and gained five more. So also, the one with the two talents gained two more.

MATTHEW 25:16 – 17

We are created by a creative God who encourages inno-vation and artistry, and commands that we exercise wise stewardship over the resources he has given us.

INTRODUCTION

The misnamed "Dark Ages" established what would become the freest and most technologically advanced civilizations in history. Christianity played a crucial role in their development.

In his book *From Plato to NATO*, historian David Gress shares the story of Cassiodorus, a sixth-century Roman nobleman who, after the fall of Rome, "proposed to the pope that they jointly found a college of higher learning in Rome, which would preserve Christian and secular literature, philosophy, and religious writings." But the dream was not meant to be. Soon another war ravaged Italy and, by the time it was over, Roman civilization lay in ruins. As an old man, Cassiodorus "wrote his last book in 580. Not a book of philosophy, ethical reflection, elevated theology, or literature, it was instead a book on spelling, because the monks had told him that they could no longer read the theological works in their own library nor could they set down their own thoughts."

At this point it would have been tempting for men and women like Cassiodorus to have simply given up on Western civilization, but they didn't. Samuel Gregg describes what followed:

> One of the great ironies of history at this particular period, one of the great comic reversals, is that this little band of monks — and not just this particular band, but monks all through Western Europe — not only did they engage in this civilizational enterprise of recapturing and reclaiming what had been lost from the classical period, they also went on together with the inventors and the merchants and the lawyers of the Middle Ages to go forward and build a culture that was going to surpass anything that had existed before it.

Sadly, the so-called "Dark Ages" are often depicted in history books as a time when immoral priests manipulated ignorant peasants, and superstitious monks retreated to barren monasteries where they wasted their talents in a spiritual escape from the "real world." But these popular stereotypes miss the real story. The period after Rome's collapse was a difficult and challenging time, but historians now recognize that the period from the fall of Rome to the invention of the printing press was really a time of profound innovation and progress, a time when Christian ideas worked their way deep into the fabric of European society.

VIDEO TEACHING NOTES

The history of the Christian West is one of faith completing reason.

Medieval Europe began to flourish after key biblical truths sank into the bones of the culture.

Capitalism first took root in the monasteries and city-states of northern medieval Italy.

Medieval Europe advanced an array of technologies.

The Dutch and English economies took off when they learned to protect and respect property rights. Now property owners had confidence to think long term, to plan, cultivate, and innovate.

Michael Novak notes that Chinese scholars determined that Christianity was a key reason medieval Europe leapt forward.

VIDEO DISCUSSION

1. According to Rodney Stark and others in this video session, in what
    ways did the European civilization of the Middle Ages eventually surpass
    anything that had come before it? What specific ideas drawn from Chris-
    tianity helped spur economic and technological progress during this time?

2. Samuel Gregg noted that economies flourished among the medieval
    Dutch and English when secure property rights emboldened farmers and
    others to think long term about their property and to use property for
    business collateral.
    a. Consider what it would be like if you could not own anything. Your
        home and your property belonged to another, as well as any profit you
        might make from investing your resources. Would you be as motivated
        to care for it, to invest in it when you knew you wouldn't see the return
        on that investment? How does the right to property encourage respon-
        sible stewardship of resources?

    b. What strategies does this suggest for helping the poor in developing
        countries today?

3. The legendary Robin Hood is often held up as a medieval English hero who "steals from the rich and gives to the poor." What's often forgotten is that Robin Hood "steals" from corrupt English noblemen who plundered hard-working peasants. In essence, he is helping to return stolen wealth to its rightful owners. Now read 2 Samuel 12:1–12 where the prophet Nathan tells King David a parable in order to prick David's conscience. What does this parable have in common with the legend of Robin Hood? What do both stories suggest about how we should treat the poor?

"*In* the image of God created he him; male and female created he them.... It is observable that in the passage leading up to the statement about man, [the author of Genesis] had given no detailed information about God. Looking at man, he sees in him something essentially divine, but when we turn back to see what he says about the original upon which the 'image' of God was modeled, we find only the single assertion, 'God created.' The characteristic common to God and man is apparently that: the desire and ability to make things."

Dorothy Sayers, *The Whimsical Christian*

4. It's not just "creative types" who are made in the image of our Creator God; we are all designed to be creative. What are some of the ways in which we express this creativity? That is, what are some specific things you are currently doing or can begin doing this week to cultivate your particular patch of God's creation?

5. Advertising executive Leo Burnett once said, "When you reach for the stars you may not quite get one, but you won't come up with a handful of mud either." Does Christianity encourage such striving and ambition? Explain.

How can we strive for excellence while also cultivating Christian contentment? How are you managing this in your own life?

Did the apostle Paul compromise between these two things, or did his life in Christ allow him to transcend the tension between ambition and contentment? Discuss this in the context of Philippians 4:11–12, 1 Timothy 6:6–7, Colossians 3:23, Philippians 3:10–14, and Romans 15:20. If any stories about Paul from the book of Acts strikes you as relevant, bring those into the discussion as well.

BONUS STUDY

If your group has time, you may choose to watch the bonus sections of the video for session three now. (If not, consider viewing them on your own or as a group as part of your between-sessions activities.) Here are some reflection questions for the additional video shorts:

1. In the first video short, Samuel Gregg reminds us that sometimes we make the mistake of thinking we're wiser than people who lived in ages past simply because we have greater scientific and techno-logical riches than they had. This mistaken attitude is often made worse by a modern culture obsessed by youth and the latest fads: past ages are stupid because they wear funny clothes and are, well, old. Have you been guilty of this prejudice against the past? What are the dangers for the church if we accept this cultural bias against the past?

2. The second video short compares the inventions of the Middles Ages to the technology of the preceding Roman Empire. Glenn Sunshine points out that the inventions of the Middle Ages did much to elevate the lot of the common peasant. What idea or ideas from Scripture does he suggest encouraged this?

3. According to the third video short, the Chinese industrial revolu-tion of the tenth century AD began with great promise but then was derailed. What happened? Is there a lesson in this for us today?

4. Many people assume that economics is an invention of the Enlight-enment. According to the fourth video short, what were some of the economic insights made by Christian scholars *before* the Enlightenment?

CLOSING PRAYER

As you close this session, here are some ways you can pray in tune with the themes of today's study:

- Ask God to help you be a wise steward of the gifts, talents, and resources that he has given you. As the apostle Paul wrote, "For we are God's workmanship, created in Christ Jesus to do good works, which God prepared in advance for us to do" (Ephesians 2:10).

- Pray that God would fill you with a spirit of creativity in the work he has given you, that you would be able to bring him honor and glory through your efforts.

- Pray that God would bless and multiply your investments of time, energy, and financial resources, and that he would grant you increasing freedom to bless others through your investments. Remember these words of Genesis 1:28a: "God blessed them and said to them, 'Be fruitful and increase in number; fill the earth and subdue it.'"

SESSION *Four*

PILGRIMS' PROGRESS

We have already made the charge that Jews and Gentiles alike are all under sin. As it is written: "There is no one righteous, not even one; there is no one who understands, no one who seeks God."

ROMANS 3:9B – 11

Because we are sinners, we need the law of God to show us what is right and to reveal our sinful capacity for evil. True freedom is found not in choosing whatever we want, but in choosing what is right and good.

INTRODUCTION

The governments of the early American colonists were shaped by the Christian drama, a story stretching from the garden of Eden and the fall, to the cross, and the eventual return of Christ described in Revelation. It's a story of creatures made in the image of God but darkened by sin, sold as slaves to sin, but called to live as sons of God and brothers of the King of Kings.

It's a heritage that some schoolchildren learn little about. Take Thanksgiving. Some schoolbooks explain that this autumn holiday began when the American pilgrims thanked some helpful Indians by inviting them to a feast. Well, hopefully the early pilgrims were grateful to generous Indians such as Squanto. But the name of the holiday comes from giving thanks to God.

We see the religious quality of the holiday prominently underscored in a presidential proclamation by George Washington a century and a half after the first Thanksgiving:

> Whereas it is the duty of all nations to acknowledge the providence of Almighty God, to obey His will, to be grateful for His benefits, and humbly to implore His protection and favor; and Whereas both Houses of Congress have, by their joint committee, requested me to *"recommend to the people of the United States a day of public thanksgiving and prayer, to be observed by acknowledging with grateful hearts the many and signal favors of Almighty God, especially by affording them an opportunity peaceably to establish a form of government for their safety and happiness:"*
>
> Now, therefore, I do recommend and assign Thursday, the 26th day of November next, to be devoted by the people of these States to the service of that great and glorious Being who is the beneficent author of all the good that was, that is, or that will be. (emphasis added)

This is just one of countless historical documents illustrating the religious underpinnings of the "American experiment." American history textbooks shouldn't sweep this stuff under the rug. The First Amendment insists that Congress make no law establishing a religion; it doesn't say that public schools must pretend that religious ideas and institutions never played a positive role in America's history. To do so is to grossly misrepresent the past. The history of the American colonies was shaped by Christian ideas from the beginning. The early settlers' understanding of God and man, good and evil, providence and depravity, helped to lay the groundwork for the most successful experiment in political liberty the world has ever seen.

VIDEO TEACHING NOTES

Because of their Christian theology, the pilgrims were acutely aware of human sinfulness. This shaped how they designed their governments.

The pilgrims emphasized that we are "image bearers" of God. This also guided their political experiments.

The political ideas the pilgrims brought to the New World had deep roots in the Christianity of the Old World.

The U.S. Declaration of Independence grounds human rights in the creation story.

The American founders took human sinfulness into account by establishing a system of checks and balances.

The American founders believed that freedom for excellence was the only kind of freedom that could last.

VIDEO DISCUSSION

1. John Witte Jr. says that early English settlers saw the Christian not only as a sinner, but also as a saint — an "image bearer of God." How did each of these ideas — our sinful capacity for evil and our potential for greatness as creations of God — influence their view of the citizen's role in the governments they established?

2. The American Declaration of Independence reads, "We hold these truths to be self-evident, that all men are created equal, that they are endowed by their Creator with certain unalienable Rights, that among these are Life, Liberty and the pursuit of Happiness. That to secure these rights, Governments are instituted among Men, deriving their just powers from the consent of the governed." According to Susan Wise Bauer, where does this "self-evident" truth come from?

   How would *you* argue that all people are created equal, if someone challenged that truth? How would you defend the idea that people have basic human rights?

3.   When Israel asked the prophet Samuel for a king, God warned them that
     it would go badly for them, but they were so enamored of the pomp and
     power of the foreign kings nearby that they wouldn't listen (see 1 Samuel
     8). Their demand was eventually granted. Look at a few representative
     examples of the result:

Scripture	Example	Failure
1 Kings 12:1–14	King Rehoboam	
1 Kings 21:1–16	King Ahab	
2 Kings 21:1–16	King Manasseh	

How did Israel's experiment in centralized, royal authority work out for
them?

What are some of the lessons we can draw from their mistakes?

4.   The American founders emphasized the need for checks and balances in
     government. According to this video session, why did they think them
     necessary? What are some of the checks and balances, and how effective
     are they?

"*Power* tends to corrupt and absolute power corrupts
absolutely."

                                                    Lord Acton

5. This video session quotes American founder George Mason from the Virginia Declaration of Rights of 1776: "Religion, or the duty which we owe to our Creator, and the manner of discharging it, can be directed only by reason and conviction, not by force or violence." What is the difference between legislating moral laws and forcing religious belief? How do we determine the difference?

6. Read Luke 9:51–56. Why do you think Jesus directed his disciples to lead people to him through evangelism and example rather than through force?

   What does this teach us about our own approach to sharing our faith?

7. The Pilgrims and the American founders emphasized that sustained liberty required virtue and self-discipline. They believed that wise self-government actually brings about greater freedom.
   a. Consider how this is true when applied to a marriage relationship. How does the decision to be with only one person lead to greater freedom? How would a married person's decision to "play the field" ultimately impair his freedom in his relationship, as well as the freedom of his family?

b. In what other situations can a measure of moral discipline—a decision to forego certain possibilities—actually expand and enhance freedom?

> "If only there were evil people somewhere insidiously committing evil deeds, and it were necessary only to separate them from the rest of us and destroy them. But the line dividing good and evil cuts through the heart of every human being."
>
> Aleksandr Solzhenitsyn

8. Philosopher Peter Kreeft contrasts *objective* good and *subjective* good. What is the danger if each of us pursues only what subjectively feels right, and where do you see evidence of this problem in our culture today?

BONUS STUDY

If your group has time, you may choose to watch the bonus sections of the video for session four now. (If not, consider viewing them on your own or as a group as part of your between-sessions activities.) Here are some reflection questions for the additional video shorts:

1. The first video short looks at how Reformed communities in sixteenth- and seventeenth-century Europe influenced the American Revolution a century later. What are some ideas from these Reformed communities that resurfaced in the American founding?

2. The second video short debunks the notion that the principle of religious toleration came to us from outside of Christianity, purely from secular thinkers. According to this video, which biblical teachings encourage religious toleration?

3. According to the third video short, what ideas did the Anabaptists and Quakers promote that contributed to the cause of liberty? Do you find this an easy way to behave?

4. To throw light on the early Christian attitude toward state power, Rodney Stark repeats a joke the church father Augustine once told: "What's the difference between an emperor and a pirate? The emperor has a much bigger navy." Stark tells this story to illustrate Christianity's long established distrust of governmental authority — distrust which began when the young church was persecuted by the Empire. Is there such a thing as a healthy distrust of government? Given that the apostle Paul instructs us to obey the governing authorities (Romans 13:1–7), how far should such a healthy distrust extend?

CLOSING PRAYER

As you close this session, here are some ways you can pray in tune with the themes of today's study:

- Pray that God would help you recognize your own tendency toward evil and reveal your need for Christ through the law. Recall these words from James 2:12: "Speak and act as those who are going to be judged by the law that gives freedom."

- Ask God to bless our leaders and those in government with wisdom and moral guidance, that they would make decisions that honor him and invite his blessing.

- Ask God to help you cultivate a spirit of self-discipline and allow you to experience the freedom that comes from choosing what is right and good.

SESSION *Five*

THE ABOLITIONISTS

Were you a slave when you were called? Don't let it trouble you—although if you can gain your freedom, do so. For he who was a slave when he was called by the Lord is the Lord's freedman.

1 CORINTHIANS 7:21 – 22A

God does not want us to live in slavery, either physical or spiritual, but encourages us to pursue and promote the cause of freedom, standing up for the oppressed and strengthening the weak.

INTRODUCTION

When slavery returned to Western civilization in the sixteenth century, men and women animated by Christian ideas led the struggle to abolish it.

The cause was a long and difficult one. Even many regular churchgoers found handy excuses for owning and abusing their fellow human beings. Of course, you don't have to be an abusive eighteenth-century slave owner to ignore somebody's human rights. While we may not actively oppress anyone, our inclination to sin, and our tendency to rationalize that sin, make it all too easy for us to ignore our responsibilities toward those who cannot defend themselves, toward those around us who are being abused and destroyed.

In the United States, the unborn lack the most basic of human rights, the right to life. And around the world today, millions of people work for employers who threaten them with violence if they try to escape. Sometimes the person is a prostitute or beggar kidnapped as a child and forced into business. Other times the person is a laborer tricked into entering a large plantation they have no freedom to ever leave. These are men, women, and children for whom freedom is only a distant dream. They need the body of Christ to speak and act on their behalf.

The good news is that the Word of God offers powerful resources for speaking prophetically against human oppression. The Bible exhorts a slave owner to treat his returning slave as a brother in Christ (Philemon 16–17). It encourages Christian slaves to obtain their freedom if they can, since "he who was a slave when he was called by the Lord is the Lord's freedman" (1 Corinthians 7:22). It reminds us that every human is made in the image of God (Genesis 1:27). It insists that "God so loved the world"—not just my tribe or my ethnic group or my nation—but "so loved the *world* that he gave his one and only son" (John 3:16). And it insists that because of this, "there is no Greek or Jew, circumcised or uncircumcised, barbarian, Scythian, slave or free, but Christ is all, and is in all" (Colossians 3:11).

William Wilberforce and Frederick Douglass, Harriet Beecher Stowe and Harriet Tubman—these abolitionists had something in common: they were Christians who put to heroic use the prophetic power of the Word to argue against the trafficking and murder of human souls. Their heritage is our heritage. Their gospel is our gospel.

VIDEO TEACHING NOTES

Medieval Europe got rid of slavery, but it returned in the age of exploration.

When the U.S. Constitution was completed, a contradiction lay at the heart of the new nation.

In the battle to end the English slave trade, William Wilberforce was persistent and prophetic but also shrewd.

In the United States, the persuasive efforts of Frederick Douglass, Harriet Tubman, Harriet Beecher Stowe, and other Christian abolitionists helped to build public support for the emancipation of the slaves.

VIDEO DISCUSSION

1. Near the beginning of this video session, the narrator describes William
    Wilberforce as an "unlikely hero." What about the young man made him
    an "unlikely hero" in the great moral crusade that lay before him?

> "*Sir,* when we think of eternity, and of the future consequences
> of all human conduct, what is there in this life that should make
> any man contradict the dictates of his conscience, the principles of
> justice, the laws of religion, and of God. Sir, the nature and all the
> circumstances of this [slave] trade are now laid open to us; we can
> no longer plead ignorance."
>
> William Wilberforce

2. God has a long track record of choosing and using "unlikely heroes."
    Consider, for example, Moses and David. Look up the Scripture listed in
    the table below and share what it was that made each seem an "unlikely
    hero." Then look at the other Scripture to find out what overlooked quali-
    ties God saw and nurtured in them.

Biblical Hero	What Made Him Unlikely?	Overlooked Quality
Moses	Exodus 4:10	Numbers 12:3
David	1 Samuel 17:32–33	Acts 13:22

3. After meeting with failure in Parliament, Wilberforce adopted a more incremental approach as well as some clever political tactics. He believed that one could possess integrity and courage while also being prudent and shrewd. Do you believe that acting this way is consistent with being a Christian? Why or why not?

When is shrewdness justifiable? When is it really just an excuse for compromising one's integrity? How do we discern the difference?

Read Matthew 10:16 where Jesus advocates shrewdness as well as integrity. Why does he say shrewdness is necessary? How can we be both wise and innocent?

4. Slavery may seem like a relic of a past era, but sadly, it is a thriving business in many parts of the world today. According to the International Justice Mission, more men, women, and children are held in slavery right now than over the course of the entire trans-Atlantic slave trade, and trafficking in humans generates profits in excess of twelve billion dollars a year. Nearly two million children are exploited in the commercial sex industry.

    a. Based on what you have learned in this session, what are the underlying beliefs and ideas that lead to the evil of slavery?

b. What are some ways that we as Christians can stand against this evil? What lessons can we learn from the abolition movement?

5. At the end of this session, host Dave Stotts asks the question: "Is there anyone that I treat as an unperson?" More broadly, is there a category of person that contemporary society encourages you to treat as less than fully human, as less than a creature made in the image of God? Answer as honestly as you can.

> "*There* are those who argue that the right to privacy is of a higher order than the right to life. That was the premise of slavery. You could not protest the existence or treatment of slaves on the plantation because that was private and therefore out of your right to be concerned. Don't let the pro-choicers convince you that a fetus isn't a human being. That's how the whites dehumanized us.... The first step was to distort the image of us as human beings in order to justify what they wanted to do—and not even feel they'd done anything wrong."
>
> Rev. Jesse Jackson, prior to his 1984 run for national political office (Nat Hentoff, *Jewish World Review*, June 12, 2006)

BONUS STUDY

If your group has time, you may choose to watch the bonus sections of the video for session five now. (If not, consider viewing them on your own or as a group as part of your between-sessions activities.) Here are some reflection questions for the additional video shorts:

1. Some scholars claim that the abolition of the English slave trade was inevitable. They argue that impersonal economic forces or some other impersonal historical dynamic was at work, and that Wilberforce's courageous moral leadership wasn't necessary. Such arguments often are based on philosophical materialism, a worldview that sees all of us as the products and playthings of impersonal forces. After watching the first video short, discuss how Wilberforce might have behaved differently if he had adopted such a philosophy of life.

2. Why did Wilberforce have such a difficult time persuading England — a "Christian nation" — to end the slave trade? Shouldn't it have been obvious to them that capturing Africans and selling them into slavery was evil? In the second video short, Glenn Sunshine explains that for most people in England at the time, "religion was just simply part of a comfortable background that they lived in." In other words, they didn't let their Christianity inconvenience them. Can you think of other instances when Christians have been guilty of accommodating evil for the sake of convenience? Where might this be true today?

3. In the third video short, William Allen explains that Frederick Douglass understood freedom as more than simply freedom from restraint. Douglass had a positive understanding of freedom, what some have called freedom for excellence. How did this richer understanding of freedom guide Douglass? Which understanding of freedom seems to dominate our culture today?

CLOSING PRAYER

As you close this session, here are some ways you can pray in tune with the themes of today's study:

- Pray for those trapped in physical slavery, for the innocent who soon may be denied the right to life, and for those who are denying other people their basic human rights.

- Pray that your congregation will become a greater force for liberation locally and abroad, bringing the good news and love of Christ into lives marked by physical or spiritual bondage.

- Pray also about any aspects of your daily walk still given over to spiritual bondage. Ask God to free you and those you live and work with from bondage to any destructive patterns of behavior that persist in your life (e.g., worry, fits of anger, overeating). Be encouraged by these words of the apostle Paul: "It is for freedom that Christ has set us free. Stand firm, then, and do not let yourselves be burdened again by a yoke of slavery" (Galatians 5:1).

SESSION *Six*

A TALE OF TWO REVOLUTIONS

The fool says in his heart, "There is no God."

PSALM 14:1

True liberty is not found by rejecting God and establishing our own rules and laws. Freedom is a blessing from God, a gift that we experience when we recognize his moral authority over our lives.

INTRODUCTION

The French Revolution rejected Christianity, and tyranny filled the moral vacuum left in its absence. The American experiment, on the other hand, appealed to a divine moral order and discovered the blessings of liberty.

In the classic nineteenth-century Russian novel *The Brothers Karamazov* by Orthodox Christian author Fyodor Dostoyevsky, one of the brothers argues that if there is no God, then there is no higher morality and anything goes. Everything is permitted.

In the novel, the idea leads to tragedy, just as it did in the French Revolution, and just as it would in Nazi Germany, the Soviet Union, and the killing fields of communist Cambodia. In these experiments, millions were slaughtered by regimes that believed there was no God in heaven to whom they were accountable. In the absence of God, these tyrants believed they were free to become their own gods and create their own morality.

The 1989 film *Crimes and Misdemeanors* plays out a similar theme, but on a smaller scale. In the film, an eye doctor has his mistress killed in order to maintain his façade as an upright, moral, family man. Though he has some pangs of guilt over committing murder, they eventually pass, and he returns to his comfortable life. Sometime later, he shares his story as a hypothetical tale with a man he meets at a friend's wedding. The stranger finds the tale quite unsatisfying, insisting that a good story would find the murderer ruined by guilt, ready to turn himself in to the authorities. The eye doctor dismisses his suggestions as unrealistic, and returns to his happy, privileged life. The film's premise is clear enough: We don't live in a just universe governed by a just God; we live in an anything-goes universe.

As this mind-set grows more common, one is left to wonder if our culture is losing the moral framework needed to sustain ordered liberty. For Christians called to be salt and light, here surely is work.

VIDEO TEACHING NOTES

The French Revolution eventually set itself against religion and ended in disaster.

The leading American founders appealed to Judeo-Christian principles in their struggle for liberty.

Christianity's insistence on an absolute standard of morality has played a crucial role in nurturing and sustaining liberty and human rights.

The cathedral of Notre Dame and the Great Arch of La Défense embody two distinct visions of European culture and of the foundations of Western freedom.

VIDEO DISCUSSION

1. Psalm 14:1 says, "The fool says in his heart, 'There is no God.'" But many
    today insist that belief in God is a matter of blind faith, not of faith com-
    pleting reason.

    a. How is denying God not merely mistaken, but deeply unreasonable —
    even foolish?

    b. What reasons would you give if someone asked you why you believe in
    God?

2. Many dismiss Christianity because they say most Christians don't actually
    live out what they believe. Of course, we should always strive to reflect
    Christ through word and deed, but even a hypocritical Christian still
    believes in a standard of judgment. Christians are not moral relativists.
    "That's the difference," Samuel Gregg says. "Christianity gives people ...
    the capacity to critique ourselves, to critique our behavior, and to design
    better institutions" in the course of striving to live up to God's standards
    of right and wrong.

    a. How does Christianity give us a basis for critiquing behavior, both in
    ourselves and in our governments and institutions?

    b. How might you respond to someone who says that Christians are "a
    bunch of hypocrites"?

> "*Liberty* cannot be established without morality, nor morality without faith."
>
> Alexis de Tocqueville, *Democracy in America*

3. Both the American Revolution and the French Revolution had their internal problems. But the American Revolution led to increasing freedom and stability, while the French Revolution descended into a series of bloody internal purges followed by a dictatorship. What was it that made the difference between the two revolutions?

4. George Washington and other American founders emphasized the connection between liberty and morality. The apostle Peter wrote, "A man is a slave to whatever has mastered him" (2 Peter 2:19b). Read this verse in context (2 Peter 2:10b–19). What evils were mastering the people Peter is describing?

What things often master us today? What resources do we as Christians have for breaking free of these things and remaining free of them?

5. William Allen argues that there "has been a systematic campaign to reinterpret our past as if it meant to disallow free expression of religion." Robert George then points out how impoverished our culture would be if Christians had not been free to make public religious arguments in support of various human rights. What are some concrete ways that Christian principles have made life today freer and more dignified?

6. Governments that ignore divine wisdom fail. Read Proverbs 14:12. What are some resources we have for avoiding paths that seem right but lead to destruction and death? How do you practice discernment in your own life, to avoid the way that "leads to death"?

"*Modern* man reinterprets liberty as he reinterprets happiness. Liberty is no longer freedom *to* attain my true, objective end, but freedom *from* obstacles and frustrations to my subjective desires."

Peter Kreeft, *Love Is Stronger Than Death*

7. Host Dave Stotts concludes this video session by discussing a poem by William Butler Yeats, written near the close of World War I, about Western culture losing its moorings:

    Turning and turning in the widening gyre
    The falcon cannot hear the falconer;
    Things fall apart; the centre cannot hold;
    Mere anarchy is loosed upon the world,
    The blood-dimmed tide is loosed, and everywhere
    The ceremony of innocence is drowned.

Stott asks, "Can modern culture still hear the falconer? Can it hear Christ? And as the body of Christ, how are we doing as his mouth and hands and arms, as his body reaching out to a lost and suffering world?" Apply this final question both individually and congregationally. Discuss the positive side of the picture and consider: How could we be doing better?

BONUS STUDY

If your group has time, you may choose to watch the bonus sections of the video for session six now. (If not, consider viewing them on your own or as a group as part of your between-sessions activities.) Here are some reflection questions for the additional video shorts:

1. In the first video short, William Allen argues that a key reason the American Revolution succeeded while the French Revolution descended into anarchy was that the United States had the moral leadership of George Washington. Allen comments:

   When George Washington in the first inaugural says to the people of the United States that there could be no public happiness without private morality, he says what sounds like a counterintuitive thing. You would think, "We get a sound state, then people can be decent." He said, "No, you've got it backwards. A sound state depends on a decent people." Nobody ever said anything like that in France.

   a. Governments can successfully minimize things such as murder through criminal codes and law enforcement. So why can't we legislate our way to a decent people? In other words, how would you defend President Washington's culture-first emphasis?

b. Even many who emphasize the primacy of culture believe that what a government declares to be illegal (laws against addictive narcotics, for instance) can influence people's sense of what is immoral. Do you agree or disagree? In other words, is there a teaching function to the law?

2. According to the second video short, the American founders hoped to protect religious liberty through the First Amendment clause, not stifle its expression. As William Allen puts it, "It never was an amendment that was designed to create freedom *from* religion. It was to create freedom *of* religion." What evidence do William Allen and Alan Crippen give? Do you find their arguments compelling?

3. In the third video short, Michael Miller discusses the nineteenth-century French political thinker Alexis de Tocqueville and his warnings about soft despotism in his famous work *Democracy in America*. Do you see signs of soft despotism in our culture today? What are some habits and virtues we must guard in order to preserve liberty?

4. In the fourth video short, Greg Forster discusses a challenge facing the United States today: Though we are properly committed to religious liberty, as a religiously diverse nation, our country's citizens no longer share a broad moral framework. What are some ways that Christians can be part of the solution to this problem without compromising religious liberty, including the freedom of others to express their own religious views?

5. Christians should abhor "hate crimes" — crimes committed because the perpetrator hates a particular group of people, of which the victim is a member. But many argue that hate crimes should not be considered a separate category of crime, because that would penalize people not only for their evil actions, but for their attitudes. What is the danger if we begin to criminalize thoughts or attitudes? How can we as Christians most effectively combat hate crimes?

CLOSING PRAYER

As you close this session, here are some ways you can pray in tune with the themes of today's study:

- Ask the Holy Spirit to impress upon you more deeply that the greatest freedom is found in total commitment to the will of God in your life.

- Pray that your nation and its leaders understand that freedom without morality cannot endure. As 1 Peter 2:16 says, "Live as free men, but do not use your freedom as a cover-up for evil; live as servants of God."

- Pray for Christian revival in your community and nation.

SESSION *Seven*

RELATIVISM VS. RELIGION

You are the light of the world. A city on a hill cannot be hidden. Neither do people light a lamp and put it under a bowl. Instead they put it on its stand, and it gives light to everyone in the house.

MATTHEW 5:14 – 15

A purpose of our freedom is to show the goodness of God by serving others in love. Those who live in the freedom of God are a light on a hill, a witness to the one who has set them free.

INTRODUCTION

Freedom and progress in the West were not founded on moral relativism or a secular Enlightenment. Freedom and progress were born out of a culture deeply interpenetrated by the Christian worldview.

To hear some people tell it, the only way we will experience freedom and progress in our diverse, globally connected economy is by embracing the sort of moral relativism that keeps religious convictions and morals outside of the public sphere. In this scenario, secularism functions as the playing field for the various faiths, determining the boundaries and limits of religious expression in public life. Moral values become a private matter.

But there's a problem with this, even aside from what the Bible teaches. In his books *Mere Christianity* and *The Abolition of Man*, C. S. Lewis points out the fundamental flaw of moral relativism. First, he concedes that there are cultural variations about what is considered "Decent Behavior." Still, he says, cultures around the world have always agreed on certain key points; for instance, courage has always been esteemed and cowardice deplored. Then Lewis comments:

> The most remarkable thing is this. Whenever you find a man who says he does not believe in a real Right and Wrong, you will find the same man going back on this a moment later. He may break his promise to you, but if you try breaking one to him he will be complaining "It's not fair" before you can say Jack Robinson. A nation may say treaties do not matter; but then, next minute, they spoil their case by saying the particular treaty they want to break was an unfair one....
>
> It seems, then, that we are forced to believe in a real Right and Wrong. People may be sometimes mistaken about them, as people sometimes get their sums wrong; but they are not a matter of mere taste and opinion any more than the multiplication table. (from *Mere Christianity*)

Christian thinkers as diverse as the apostle Paul, Thomas Aquinas, Martin Luther, and John Calvin have all emphasized that the law written on the human heart has communicated to us certain universal ground rules for human behavior. While this can be useful for establishing common ground with nonbelievers, history shows that this by itself never led to widespread freedom. This law written on the human heart led a few to promote freedom for all, but such attempts remained isolated and fitful. The efforts never gathered sufficient momentum and sweep to carry an entire civilization to widespread liberty. Something else was needed. That something else was Christianity.

VIDEO TEACHING NOTES

Moral relativism provides no basis for opposing atrocities such as the Nazi holocaust.

Violence and oppression are the norm in human history. The question for historians is how, from the base stuff of sinful humanity, freedom was born in the West.

Philosopher Alfred North Whitehead argued that Judeo-Christian ideas played a crucial role in the birth of science.

Some secularists assume that Europeans learned the principles of freedom in the seventeenth century and the subsequent history embodied by the French Revolution.

The freedom project in the modern world emerged not in China, India, or the Islamic world, but in the Christian West.

VIDEO DISCUSSION

1. You may have heard someone say that it's wrong to impose our values and beliefs on other people. After all, "what's true for you may not be true for me." Near the beginning of this video, Robert George suggests that this is actually "the worst possible way to defend the ideals of freedom and democracy." How does George defend his assertion? Do you find his argument compelling? Why or why not?

2. Rodney Stark argues that Christianity contributed to the rise of modern science. This might surprise those who believe science and religion oppose each other. How, according to Stark, did Christianity help to fuel the scientific revolution?

3. George Weigel asks, "Where did European men and women learn that they were people of inalienable or inherent dignity and value, who had a right to be consulted about how they were ruled? Where did Europe learn that the prince is also subject to the law? Where did Europe learn that there was a moral law written on the human heart, moral truths that we can know by reason? Where did Europe learn that persuasion is better than coercion in the doing of the public business?" What are the two opposing answers to his question? Which answer do the scholars in *The Birth of Freedom* give? What evidence do they offer to support their view?

"*Men* have now by nature no peace within their hearts, for God is crowned there no longer, but there in the moral dusk stubborn and aggressive usurpers fight among themselves for first place on the throne."

A. W. Tozer

4. The American founders saw a close connection between freedom and virtue. Consider a student who exercises his freedom from parental supervision by skipping classes and blowing off his assignments. After four years of such behavior, will he find himself more or less free, with more or fewer choices, than the person who bound himself to academic toil? Discuss this in the context of Proverbs 12:24. How can laziness and poor choices lead to a form of "slavery"?

"*If* anyone will take the trouble to compare the moral teaching of, say, the ancient Egyptians, Babylonians, Hindus, Chinese, Greeks and Romans, what will really strike him will be how very like they are to each other and to our own."

C. S. Lewis, *Mere Christianity*

5. Read Romans 1:18–20 and 2:14–15. Our consciences are clouded by sin and yet, as C. S. Lewis notes, there are common moral precepts shared across cultures, even by people who claim to be moral relativists. What are some of these shared moral beliefs that seem to transcend cultures?

6. Read Matthew 5:14–15. The most fundamental way that we are lights to the world is by showing people the love of Christ and sharing the gospel message. But the light of Christ is far reaching. Review some additional ways discussed in this video series that Christians and Christianity have been a light to the world.

7. As the New Testament explains, the freedom that Jesus called people to is not only freedom from guilt and the penalty of sin. Jesus also calls us to become free by becoming the people we were designed to be—divine image-bearers who are creative, generous, merciful, loving, and just. What are some ways that you have observed these qualities in the lives of people around you? How do these character qualities witness to the freedom we enjoy in Christ?

8. Recall the story of Cassiodorus from the first video session. In the face of the chaos and violence that followed the Roman Empire's collapse, he and other Christians could have given up. Instead, they patiently forged a new civilization. To appreciate the value of their efforts, do a little thought experiment: Imagine how Western civilization would be different today if all of those Christians had simply fled back to the Holy Lands and left Europe and the West to develop without Christianity. Make a list of the differences.

BONUS STUDY

If your group has time, you may choose to watch the bonus sections of the video for session seven now. (If not, consider viewing them on your own or as a group in the coming days.) Here are some reflection questions for the additional video shorts:

1. In the first video short, Robert George looks at what tends to happen when modern nations have rejected or discarded the idea that humans are made in God's image. What examples does Professor George give? What do you see as the cure for such evils?

2. In the second video short, Robert George responds to the question, "What do you say to someone who believes social progress means moving further from religion?" What might you say to such a person; where do you begin? Assume it's someone who doesn't believe that the Bible is the inspired Word of God.

3. Discuss the question posed by the third video short: "What connection did the American founders see between freedom and virtue?"

4. In the final video short, George Weigel discusses the role Christianity played in the struggle against tyranny in the twentieth century. List the examples he offers and then add any other twentieth-century examples you can think of. Do you think students are likely to learn about such things from high school history textbooks? Why or why not? Next, think of instances in the twentieth century when Christians failed to stand against tyranny. Can we learn anything from these negative examples?

5. In his 1963 "I Have a Dream" speech, Martin Luther King Jr. appealed to the biblical idea that all humans are made in God's image to argue for equal rights before the law for blacks and

whites, rich and poor. Does this remain the core emphasis of the Civil Rights movement in the United States today? What principles should be emphasized going forward?

6. A moral relativist might say, "Your religion is fine. But I have my own morality. Everyone should be able to find his own morality, his own spiritual truth." What's seductive about this approach? How would you respond to it?

7. If the idea that man is made in God's image is at the root of freedom, and if a vibrant moral culture nurtures and sustains that freedom, are there things we can do to help freedom grow in parts of the world where oppression now thrives?

CLOSING PRAYER

As you close this session, here are some ways you can pray in tune with the themes of today's study:

- Pray that in our efforts not to seem judgmental or condemning to non-Christians, we will not substitute moral relativism for the grace and love of the gospel.

- Pray that you can help moral relativists see that relativism cannot protect human rights and human dignity.

- Pray that the nations of the world will see that Christianity has been, and remains, the greatest force for human rights. Remember the promise and command found in Galatians 5:13: "You, my brothers, were called to be free. But do not use your freedom to indulge the sinful nature; rather, serve one another in love."

READING RESOURCES

Acton Institute for the Study of Religion and Liberty, www.acton.org.

Lord Acton, "The History of Freedom in Antiquity and The History of Freedom in Christianity" (1877), available at http://www.acton.org/research/acton/.

Lord Acton, *Selected Writings of Lord Acton* (3 vols.), ed. J. Rufus Fears (Liberty Fund, 1988).

William Allen, *George Washington: A Collection* (Liberty Fund, 1988).

William Allen and Kevin Cloonan, *The Federalist Papers: A Commentary* (Peter Lang, 2000).

Susan Wise Bauer, *The History of the Ancient World* (Norton, 2007).

Susan Wise Bauer, *The History of the Medieval World* (Norton, 2010).

Harold Berman, *Law and Revolution*, vols. 1 and 2 (Harvard University Press, 1983, 2003).

Alan R. Crippen II, *John Jay: An American Wilberforce?* (John Jay Institute, 2005), available at http://www.johnjayinstitute.org/index.cfm?get=get.johnjaypapers.

Christopher Dawson, *Religion and the Rise of Western Culture* (Sheed and Ward, 1951).

Fyodor Dostoyevsky, *Crime and Punishment* (1866).

The Federalist Papers (1788), available at http://www.foundingfathers.info/federalistpapers/.

Robert George, *The Clash of Orthodoxies: Law, Religion, and Morality in Crisis* (ISI Books, 2002).

Samuel Gregg, *On Ordered Liberty: A Treatise on the Free Society* (Lexington Books, 2003).

David Gress, *From Plato to NATO: The Idea of the West and Its Opponents* (Free Press, 1998).

F. A. Hayek (ed.), *Capitalism and the Historians* (University of Chicago Press, 1954).

C. S. Lewis, *The Abolition of Man* (1943).

Aleksandr Solzhenitsyn, *The Gulag Archipelago* (1973).

Rodney Stark, *For the Glory of God: How Monotheism Led to Reformations, Science, Witch-Hunts, and the End of Slavery* (Princeton University Press, 2003).

Rodney Stark, *The Victory of Reason: How Christianity Led to Freedom, Capitalism, and Western Success* (Random House, 2005).

Glenn Sunshine, *Why You Think the Way You Do: The Story of Western Worldviews from Rome to Home* (Zondervan, 2009).

Alexis de Tocqueville, *Democracy in America* (1835, 1840).

George Weigel, *The Cube and Cathedral* (Basic Books, 2005).

John Witte Jr., *Religion and the American Constitutional Experiment* (Westview Press, 2005).

ABOUT THE AUTHORS

Jonathan Witt is a research fellow at the Acton Institute and a senior fellow of Discovery Institute's Center for Science & Culture. He is the coauthor of *A Meaningful World* (InterVarsity Press, 2006) and *Intelligent Design Uncensored* (InterVarsity Press, 2010). A former professor at Lubbock Christian University, he also wrote or cowrote scripts for three documentaries that appeared on PBS: *The Privileged Planet*, *The Call of the Entrepreneur*, and *The Birth of Freedom*.

Amanda Witt is an adjunct professor of English at Cornerstone University, a freelance writer, and a homeschooling mother. She also designs invitations and cards at RiverJude.com.

Together the Witts wrote the participant's guide and the scripts for the *Effective Stewardship* video curriculum. Each earned a PhD from the University of Kansas, a master's degree from Texas A&M, and a bachelor's degree from Abilene Christian University. They live in Grand Rapids, Michigan, with their three children.

Effective Stewardship

Doing What Matters Most

Acton Institute

Christian stewardship is about more than the money we drop into the collection plate—stewardship is everything we do after we say we believe. In this five-session video study, hosted by Dave Stotts, along with the separate participant's guide, you will learn how to think critically and biblically about the areas of responsibility that have been entrusted to you by God.

- Session 1 — Our Talents and Skills: How to use our God-given talents to serve God in our daily vocation.
- Session 2 — The Environment: A proper, biblical understanding of resources and of humanity's relationship to nature, providing the basis for an environmental ethic of stewardship.
- Session 3 — Loving Our Neighbor: How to effectively care for those in need and ensure that our attempts to help do not cause more harm than good.
- Session 4 — Church and Family: How effective stewardship in our homes and in our churches strengthens the social impact of our families and faith congregations.
- Session 5 — Finances and Giving: How to be good stewards of our wealth by following time-tested principles of budgeting and wealth management.

Available in stores and online!

NIV Stewardship Study Bible

Discover God's Design for Life, the Environment, Finances, Generosity, and Eternity

New International Version

The *NIV Stewardship Study Bible* uses a variety of engaging features to lead individuals through a comprehensive study of what it means to be managers entrusted with the resources of God. Through 366 Exploring Stewardship notes, profiles of individuals, notes on challenges to stewardship, quotes on stewardship from respected Christians throughout the ages, and other articles and helps, the *NIV Stewardship Study Bible* projects a positive picture of the privilege that we have to manage what God has given us to his glory and to the building of his kingdom.

More than just money, this Bible emphasizes stewardly responsibility in all areas of life, including relationships, creation care, money management, institutions, and caring for the poor, among other areas. It's been pulled together with the purpose of changing perceptions about what the word "stewardship" means—not something intended to be draining and guilt-inducing, but rather motivating, empowering, and uplifting.

The *NIV Stewardship Study Bible* has been endorsed by Crown Ministries, Dave Ramsey, Good $ense Ministry, the Barnabas Foundation, Prison Fellowship, and various other programs and ministries that seek to encourage responsible stewardship among Christians. This Bible will be a natural "next step" for individuals and groups who benefit from these ministries and take part in their programs.

Available in stores and online!

NOTES:

Share Your Thoughts

With the Author: Your comments will be forwarded to
the author when you send them to *zauthor@zondervan.com*.

With Zondervan: Submit your review of this book
by writing to *zreview@zondervan.com*.

Free Online Resources at
www.zondervan.com

Zondervan AuthorTracker: Be notified whenever your favorite
authors publish new books, go on tour, or post an update
about what's happening in their lives at www.zondervan.com/
authortracker.

Daily Bible Verses and Devotions: Enrich your life with daily
Bible verses or devotions that help you start every morning
focused on God. Visit www.zondervan.com/newsletters.

Free Email Publications: Sign up for newsletters on Christian
living, academic resources, church ministry, fiction, children's
resources, and more. Visit www.zondervan.com/newsletters.

Zondervan Bible Search: Find and compare Bible passages in
a variety of translations at www.zondervanbiblesearch.com.

Other Benefits: Register yourself to receive online benefits
like coupons and special offers, or to participate in research.

ZONDERVAN®

ZONDERVAN.com/
AUTHORTRACKER
follow your favorite authors